EXPLORING

CROSVILLE

COUNTRY

· A PAST AND PRESENT COMPANION ·

CHESTER · ELLESMERE PORT · BIRKENHEAD

Services C3, C4

C3 via Ellesmere Port, Dock Street, Little Sutton, Eastham and Bromborough.
C4 via Ellesmere Port, Aldgate, Sutton Way, Little Sutton, Eastham and Bromborough.
Including certain journeys on Services C5 and F51.

Monday to Saturday

	C5	F51	C5 NS	C4 NS	C5	C3 NS	C3	C5 NS	C4 NS	C3	C4 NS	C3 NS	C3	C4	C3	C4		C3	C4	C3	C4
CHESTER (Bus Station)	0515	....	0615	....	0640	....	0710	....	0730	....	0745	0800	0815	0830	0845			00	15	30	45
The Bache (Egerton Arms)	0520	....	0620	....	0645	....	0715	....	0735	....	0750	0805	0820	0835	0850			05	20	35	50
Moston Hospital	0525	....	0625	....	0650	....	0720	....	0740	....	0755	0810	0825	0840	0855			10	25	40	55
Whitby (The Groves)	0533	....	0633	....	0658	....	0728	....	0748	....	0803	0818	0833	0848	0903			18	33	48	03
Whitby (Sportsman's Arms)	0537	....	0637	....	0702	....	0732	0734	0752	0759	0807	0822	0837	0852	0907			22	37	52	07
ELLESMERE PORT (Bus Stn.) arr.	0540	....	0640	....	0705	....	0735	0737	0755	0802	0810	0825	0840	0855	0910	and		25	40	55	10
ELLESMERE PORT (Bus Stn) dep.	....	0623	....	0646	....	0705	....	0741	0755	0806	0810	0825	0841	0855	0911	at		25	41	55	11
Ellesmere Port (Dock Street)	....	....	....	0641	....	0710	0730	....	0800	....	0815	0830	....	0900	these			30	...	00	... until
Aldgate (No. 20)	....	....	....	....	....	....	....	0744	....	0809	....	....	0844	0914	times			...	44	...	14
Overpool Road (Sutton Way)	....	....	....	0653	....	....	....	0748	....	0813	....	....	0848	0918	past			...	48	...	18
Overpool (Cemetery Gates)	....	0631	....	0656	....	0716	0736	0751	0806	0816	0821	0836	0851	0906	0921	each		36	51	06	21
Little Sutton (Red Lion)	....	0634	....	0659	....	0719	0739	0754	0809	0819	0824	0839	0854	0909	0924	hour		39	54	09	24
Hooton Cross Roads	....	0639	....	0704	....	0724	0744	0759	0814	0824	0829	0844	0859	0914	0929			44	59	14	29
Eastham (Bridle Road)	....	0642	....	0707	....	0727	0747	0802	0817	0827	0832	0847	0902	0917	0932			47	02	17	32
Bromborough Cross	....	0647	....	0712	....	0732	0752	0807	0822	0832	0837	0852	0907	0922	0937			52	07	22	37
New Ferry (Toll Bar)	....	0656	....	0721	....	0741	0801	0816	0831	0841	0846	0901	0916	0931	0946			01	16	31	46
Rock Ferry (Bedford Road)	....	0700	....	0725	....	0745	0805	0820	0835	0845	0850	0905	0920	0935	0950			05	20	35	50
BIRKENHEAD (Woodside)	....	0708	....	0733	....	0753	0813	0828	0843	0853	0858	0913	0928	0943	0958			13	28	43	58

	C4	C3	C4	C3	C4	C3	C4	C3 NS	C4 S	C3	C4	C3 NS	C4 S	C3	C4	S
CHESTER (Bus Station)	1845	1900	1930	2000	2030	2100	2130	2200	2200	2203	2230	2300	2300	2305	2326	
The Bache (Egerton Arms)	1850	1905	1935	2005	2035	2105	2135	2205	2205	2208	2235	2305	2305	2310	2331	
Moston Hospital	1855	1910	1940	2010	2040	2110	2140	2210	2210	2213	2240	2310	2310	2315	2336	
Whitby (The Groves)	1903	1918	1948	2018	2048	2118	2148	2218	2218	2221	2248	2318	2318	2323	2344	
Whitby (Sportsman's Arms)	1907	1922	1952	2022	2052	2122	2152	2222	2222	2225	2252	2322	2322	2327	2348	
ELLESMERE PORT (Bus Stn.) arr.	1910	1925	1955	2025	2055	2125	2155	2225	2225	2228	2255	2325	2325	2330	2351	
ELLESMERE PORT (Bus Stn) dep.	1911	1925	1956	2025	2056	2125	2156	2225	2226	2228	2256	....	2325	2331	2351	
Ellesmere Port (Dock Street)	....	1930	....	2030	....	2130	....	2230	....	2233	....	2330	....	....	....	
Aldgate (No. 20)	1914	....	1959	....	2059	....	2159	....	2229	....	2259	....	2334	2354		
Overpool Road (Sutton Way)	1918	....	2003	....	2103	....	2203	....	2233	....	2303	....	2338	2358		
Overpool (Cemetery Gates)	1921	1936	2006	2036	2106	2136	2206	2236	2236	2239	2306	....	2336	2341	0001	
Little Sutton (Red Lion)	1924	1939	2009	2039	2109	2139	2209	2239	2239	2242	2309	....	2339	2344	0004	
Hooton Cross Roads	1929	1944	2014	2044	2114	2144	2214	2244	....	2247	2314	....	2344	2349	0009	
Eastham (Bridle Road)	1932	1947	2017	2047	2117	2147	2217	2247	....	2250	2317	....	2347	2352	0012	
Bromborough Cross	1937	1952	2022	2052	2122	2152	2222	2252	....	2255	2322	....	2352	2357	0017	
New Ferry (Toll Bar)	1946	2001	2031	2101	2131	2201	2231	2301	....	2304	2331	....	0001	0006	0026	
Rock Ferry (Bedford Road)	1950	2005	2035	2105	2135	2205	2235	2305	....	2308	2335	....	●	0010	....	
BIRKENHEAD (Woodside)	1958	2013	2043	2113	2143	2213	2243	2313	....	2316	2343	....	●	0018	....	

CODE
NS—Not Saturday
S—Saturday.
⚓—Connection with Ferry Services.
⇌—Adjoining or near Railway Station.
●—Continues to Rock Ferry (Crosville Depot) arr. 2 mins. after New Ferry timing.

FOR SPECIAL CONDITIONS BETWEEN HOOTON CROSS RDS. AND BIRKENHEAD. FOR DETAILS SEE PAGE 49

ADDITIONAL JOURNEY (Schooldays only)—
1535 Backford (C of E School)—Ellesmere Port (Bus Station)

CC23/55/1486

3 July 1977

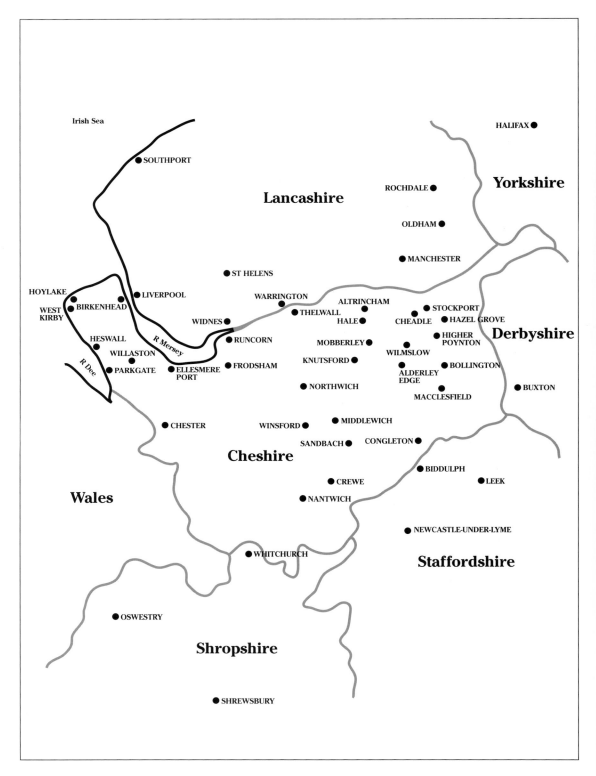

Sketch map showing places in England served by Crosville

EXPLORING

CROSVILLE

COUNTRY

· A PAST AND PRESENT COMPANION ·

Part 1: England

John Hillmer

·TOWN AND COUNTRY HERITAGE·
from
The NOSTALGIA *Collection*

First published in 2005

British Library Cataloguing in Publication Data

A catalogue record for this book is available from the British Library.

ISBN 1 85895 248 4

Past & Present Publishing Ltd
The Trundle
Ringstead Road
Great Addington
Kettering
Northants NN14 4BW

Tel/Fax: 01536 330588
email: sales@nostalgiacollection.com
Website: www.nostalgiacollection.com

Printed and bound in Great Britain

Past and
Present

A Past & Present book
from
The NOSTALGIA *Collection*

Acknowledgements

My thanks go to the following who have kindly allowed the use of their photographs and/or have been generous with their time: John Banks, Nigel Chatfield, Alistair Douglas, John Fozard, Chris Heaps, Malcolm Jones, Neville Knight, Kevin Lane, Chris Lodington, Keith Mason, Tony Moyes, Peter Thompson, Gwyn Taylor-Williams, Bryan Wilson, John Young for all his help in identifying non-Crosville vehicles, Paul Shannon for the map, my wife Geraldine for her expertise in digital scanning and printing, and Will Adams at Silver Link for his help and advice. John Robinson kindly read the manuscript, making very constructive suggestions, and I am particularly grateful to him, hastening to add that the responsibility for any errors that may remain is totally mine. I am also grateful for assistance from Cheshire & Chester Archives & Local Studies, Neston Library, and the Tourist Information offices at Piece Hall in Halifax and Runcorn.

Right BIRKENHEAD: In the red and yellow livery of PMT, Leyland Olympian DOG 115 (KFM 115X) leaves the new bus station on Service 72 to Heswall and Arrowe Park on 29 August 1991. It is still carrying the Crosville name on the front, following transfer to PMT on 3 February 1990. New to Crosville in 1982, the chassis was actually built at Bristol Commercial Vehicles, despite the Leyland badge. *JCH*

Contents

CHESTER: Looking east, this wonderful photograph shows Chester Corporation tram No 8 operating to Saltney with Crosville all-Leyland Lion 200 (FM 4334) alongside. This bus entered service in 1927, lasting until 1941. The first trams ran from Saltney to General station in 1903, continuing until 1930, when they were replaced by buses.

Today, although there is some vehicular access, normally no buses pass under the bridge. The area is partly pedestrianised, but the buildings appear to be much the same despite the passage of time to 18 May 2004. *John Banks Collection/JCH*

Introduction

Crosville was greatly loved, and few bus companies have been so carefully documented and written about. It speaks for itself that the Crosville Enthusiasts Club survives more than 15 years after the company ceased to exist, publishing a monthly 'Review' that keeps members abreast of news of ex-Crosville vehicles and covers the areas now operated by Arriva, First, et al.

In general, in compiling this book, the old pre-1974 county boundaries have been used so that, for instance, Warrington and Widnes return temporarily to Lancashire. Most of the photographs have not been previously published. As the majority of Crosville buses had bodies by Eastern Coach Works (ECW), this is not mentioned unless otherwise stated.

Hopefully this book will offer something a little different – a commemoration of the Crosville territory. The company grew partly naturally, partly through acquisition, partly through having firms like North Western handed to it, until in the end Crosville buses could be seen from Liverpool to Manchester and Rochdale, extending as far as Halifax in West Yorkshire, down to Macclesfield in Cheshire, into Staffordshire and Shropshire, then virtually the whole of North and Mid Wales, eventually reaching down as far as Newcastle Emlyn and beyond into South West Wales.

My first introduction to Crosville was in the early 1950s when I was a National Serviceman stationed at RAF Hawarden, then in 1972, when Crosville's green buses appeared in my home town of Wilmslow for the first time after North Western was split up. In this book we look at England, where Crosville began life in Chester. Sadly there are now few signs that the company ever existed, but the memories will linger on for many years to come. I hope readers will get the same pleasure from the book as I did in its preparation.

John Hillmer
Wilmslow, Cheshire

The development of Crosville territory in England

Founded in Chester in 1906 with car assembly in mind, it was 1911 before Crosville's first bus service was started from Chester to Ellesmere Port. Expansion came in 1913 when services commenced between Crewe and Nantwich, Crewe and Middlewich, and Chester to New Ferry, followed the same year by a foothold gained by services into Crewe town after the purchase of an established business. It was in 1919, after the end of the First World War, that services to Hoole were started, then from New Ferry to Meols, the same year bringing West Kirby and Hoylake into the system. By the end of that year Crosville was serving Helsby, Frodsham, Runcorn and Warrington, all from Chester, together with a Chester-Hoole circular. Despite problems with the municipal operators on the Wirral, licences to operate from West Kirby to Wallasey Village were granted by 1920; however, Birkenhead Corporation prevented Crosville from entering the town. Access to Liverpool was an important goal, and in 1922 services commenced from Widnes to Speke, Garston, Penketh and Warrington, but it was

1925 before agreement was reached with Liverpool City Council for Crosville to extend its service from Widnes to Garston and into the city centre. In mid-Cheshire Crosville wanted to expand into Northwich, but the local operating company was bought by North Western Road Car Company so the opportunity was lost. Crosville was now operating an area in England covering Cheshire (including Wirral) and parts of Lancashire, as well as extensively in Wales.

In 1929 Crosville was bought by the London, Midland & Scottish Railway, but by 1930 a new company had been formed as Crosville Motor Services Ltd (CMS). By acquisition, the company continued to widen its range, including the Tarporley area. Local agreements with Birkenhead and Liverpool Corporations enabled Crosville to further expand. Following the outbreak of the Second World War, many services were cut back; hostilities also brought an end to excursions, tours, private hire etc. Re-instatements came in 1945, and the next few years were extremely busy, but by 1950 the post-war boom was subsiding and there was a reduction in passenger journeys. Contraction of services continued and there was additional trimming back in rural Cheshire. By 1 January 1969, as part of the National Bus Company (NBC), Crosville benefited from the break-up of North Western in 1972, which brought depots in Northwich, Macclesfield and Biddulph into the fold.

In 1986 the four largest NBC companies were considered too large and were split up, into two in the case of Crosville, with the Welsh operations (plus Oswestry) being formed into a new NBC company, Crosville Wales Ltd. On 21 December 1987 this was sold to a management team. The following year, on 25 March 1988, Crosville passed into the private sector as a subsidiary of ATL. There was one unexpected short-lived expansion when fellow group member Yelloway of Rochdale, following years of decline, was handed to Crosville, but by 1990 the latter had been dismantled, bringing to an end nearly 80 years of bus operation in England and Wales.

Bibliography

Anderson, R. C. *History of Crosville* (David & Charles)

Banks, John *Crosville – the Prestige Series* (Venture Publications)

Carroll, John and Roberts, Duncan *Crosville Motor Services, Part 1 The first 40 years* (Venture Publications)

Crosland-Taylor, W. J. *State Owned Without Tears* (Transport Publishing Co Ltd)
    The Sowing and the Harvest (Transport Publishing Co Ltd)

Maund, T. B., FCIT *Crosville on Merseyside* (Transport Publishing Co Ltd)

Maund, T. B., FCIT and Boumphrey, M. *The Wirral Country Bus* (Wirral)

Roberts, Duncan *Crosville Motor Services, Part 2 1945-1990* (NBC Books)
    Crosville Motor Services, Part 3 The Successors 1986-2001 (NBC Books)

Robinson, J. P. *Crosville – The Final Harvest* (article in *Buses Extra* 74 (Dec 91/Jan 92), Ian Allan Publishing)

Anyone interested in the Crosville Enthusiasts' Club (1967) should contact John Baker, Secretary, at Park View, 13 Wepre Lane, Connah's Quay, Flintshire CH5 4JR, email Johnbaker_007@hotmail.com.

The Club has its own web site at www.crosville-ec.org.uk

Chester and Wirral

BIRKENHEAD has a fascinating history, from the first ferry operated by monks across the Mersey to Liverpool, through shipbuilding and as a port that exported enormous quantities of bunkering coal across the world, to the building of the Mersey Tunnel. The ferries continued to prosper until the first tunnel was opened, which brought about their decline, although they continue to operate today between Birkenhead and Liverpool, returning via Seacombe. Woodside remains the ferry departure point as well as a bus station, but the railway station closed in 1967. This classic view, taken on 23 March 1983, shows the Mersey estuary behind the ferry terminal, with the view across to the Liver Buildings and Roman Catholic Cathedral in Liverpool. Bristol VR DVG 479 (WTU 479W) is leaving for Chester on Service C1, with a Leyland National on the left arriving and a host of buses in the bus station.

On 21 October 2004 the 'present' photograph shows the new bus station with a clear view of the Liverpool skyline beyond. Arriva is the main operator in the area and has a parking ground nearby. Many services call at the other principal bus station in the town, near the Market. *John Robinson/ JCH*

Bristol LWL KW228 (LFM 809), new in 1951, stands in front of the handsome train sheds of Birkenhead Woodside in June 1952, operating the Caldy Service. *John Fozard*

BIRKENHEAD: Hamilton Square has some fine examples of Victorian architecture. Leyland Olympian DOG 114 (KFM 114Y) on Service 75 waits departure to Heswall on 23 March 1983. Behind is the unusual tower above Hamilton Square railway station advertising a frequent service to Liverpool via the Mersey Tunnel; the tower originally contained the hydraulic system for operating the lifts. The town has the distinction of having introduced the first public tramway in the UK, and has a Joseph Paxton-designed park, which was instrumental in the layout of New York's Central Park.

In the 'present' picture of 21 October 2004, we can see that while the railway station tower remains, there have been other changes to several of the nearby buildings. Happy Al's Dennis Dart/Plaxton Pointer 25 (VU52 UEG) is on Route 177 to Heswall. *John Robinson/JCH*

CHESTER was the birthplace of Crosville, when the first service began to Ellesmere Port in 1911, nearly 2000 years after the Romans established their fortress Deva here! The black and white timbered buildings are a feature of the present city, as are the two-tiered shopping 'Rows'. Horse-races at the Roodee course are the most ancient in the country held at their original venue, and possibly the only one in the country where the horses run anti-clockwise. Several Crosville buses can be seen approaching the city centre along Northgate on 6 August 1960, the closest being Bristol K6B DKB 393 (KFM 269) on Service C1 from Birkenhead. The photograph was taken from the city walls looking north.

Forty-four years later, on 15 August 2004, a number of buildings are immediately recognisable, although more modern traffic lights have been added at the junction of Canal Street and George Street. Arriva Dennis Dart/East Lancs 1260 (N260 CKA) shows Service 230 but also 'Sorry not in service' on the blind. *A. J. Douglas/JCH*

CHESTER's St Werburgh Street connects Town Hall Square with Eastgate/Foregate Streets. In 1974 Bristol RE ERG 58 (UFM 58F), showing Mold Route B7 on the blinds, has just passed the Cathedral (off the picture to the right).

Despite the passage of more than 30 years the buildings show little change, although the Town Hall clock now has hands and there has been a change of lamp-post on the right. The big difference on 20 November 2004 is that there are now normally no service buses down the street. *A. Moyes/JCH*

Opposite CHESTER: On 25 October 1979 Leyland National ENL 952 (LMB 952P) on Service C75 to Waverton has just come under the famous clock on Eastgate Street, heading in an easterly direction.

On 18 May 2004 there are plenty of pedestrians about and cars are able to use the street, but no buses. The outline of the pavement has been altered but generally there has been very little change – even the W. H. Smith sign appears the same. *A. J. Douglas/JCH*

CHESTER: In Town Hall Square on a rather wet 21 May 1983, swinging into its stand is Bristol VR DVG 561 (SMS 41H). This vehicle was acquired second-hand in 1982 from Eastern National, having been new to Alexander (Midland).

No buses pass this way now. The area has been pedestrianised and a rather imposing entrance has been added, leading to the market, at the front of the rectangular building seen in the 'past' photograph. In the foreground is a very modern sculpture, on another wet day, 20 November 2004. *John Robinson/JCH*

CHESTER: When this photograph was taken in Bridge Street on 7 November 1967, buses were using the street regularly, such as Bristol FLF coach DFB 152 (AFM 115B) heading towards the City Centre. A number of services used Lower Bridge Street (seen in the distance beyond the black and white building) as their termini, including the important Wrexham/Llangollen route.

There is no through traffic now to Watergate St/Eastgate as the north end has been pedestrianised; otherwise there has been very little change in the view in the 36 years to 20 November 2004. *Chris Lodington/JCH*

CHESTER DEPOT in Liverpool Road was known as 'The Rink' due to its former use as a roller-skating rink. Opened by Crosville in 1927, it was extensively modernised in 1975. In the first photo, taken at the rear of the garage in May 1952, there is a mixture of Bristol single-deckers and Leyland double-deckers. The 'present' shot shows the view on 20 November 2004. Buses enter the depot from Victoria Road.

The third picture shows the front of the depot on 28 July 1983, with Bristol VR DVG 465 (WTU 465W) at the front, and Bristol MW recovery vehicle G386 (302 PFM) on the extreme left.

The present-day equivalent, 21 years later on 18 May 2004, shows very little change to the fabric of the depot, but the major difference is that it now belongs to First Group, following the sale to PMT in 1990 (together with the Crosville name). *All JCH*

16

CHESTER: Hoole Road is one of the main arteries in and out of the city. At the bottom of the road, looking towards Hoole and about to cross the railway bridge near the station, is Bristol LD DLB 727 (VFM 592), heading towards the City Centre on 14 October 1968 on Route C41, the Hoole circular.

The scene has changed very little, although the building on the right has lost a few chimney pots! The cheap flight poster to Malaga is a fairly recent phenomenon. On 20 November 2004 First Group Mercedes-Benz/Plaxton Beaver 50023 (R233 ERE) is working on Service 53 (C53 in Crosville days) to Kingsway. *Chris Lodington/JCH*

ELLESMERE PORT prospered with the development of the Shropshire Union Canal (planned to connect the Rivers Severn, Mersey and Dee, and opened in 1795) and later the Manchester Ship Canal. Subsequently there was a large growth of refineries and chemical works, and there is a large Vauxhall car plant nearby. At the bus station/parking ground on 10 October 1984, Bristol VR DVG 547 (UUF 116J), new to Southdown, is working on Service F63 to Hope Farm Estate. There was no depot building, and at nights/weekends buses were parked closely together around the area of the bus station.

The 'present' photo of 20 November 2004 shows the modern bus station in the town centre, which has been completely and attractively re-developed. *John Robinson/JCH*

ELLESMERE PORT: This mid-1950s photograph shows the level-crossing in Station Road over the Hooton to Helsby line, with two Bristol LD Lodekkas about to pass, both operating on Route C3 between Birkenhead and Chester. The crossing was controlled by the adjacent signal box, which subsequently closed.

The major change is that the crossing has been replaced by a substantial road bridge over the railway, officially opened in 1961 and making the original Station Road a dead end, as seen on 20 November 2004. The ornate chimney on the roof of the station building remains in situ, probably dating back to when the station was opened as Whitby Locks in 1863. Although a through station, there are only four trains a day to Helsby, but a half-hourly service in the other direction on the electrified line to Birkenhead and Liverpool. *Cheshire & Chester Archives & Local Studies/JCH*

HESWALL is a busy, mainly residential, town where many people live who work in Liverpool or Chester. It had one of the first custom-built bus stations in the North of England, opened in 1924, and the depot's normal allocation was around 30. In this Sunday morning photo of 29 January 1984, the buses are closely parked in perfect straight lines. The depot building is to the left of the vehicles.

Following closure of the garage in 1988, it was demolished and the bus station surprisingly closed too. This resulted in problems with the buses in the very busy main road, so a new bus station was built on the old site, as seen in the picture of 21 October 2004 – one or two houses in the background are recognisable. Various companies use the bus station, including First, Arriva, Avon and Happy Al's. First Volvo Olympian/Alexander 34224 (P224 MPU) is working on Route 72 to Liverpool via the Tunnel. The name 'Crosville' is still used on some of the timetables on display. *Both JCH*

PARKGATE is a delightful village by the side of the tidal Dee Estuary, although it takes a very high tide for water to reach the promenade, perhaps only twice a year. In the early part of the 18th century ships sailed from here to Ireland and were able to anchor within 50 yards of the promenade, known as The Parade. As the river silted up, gradually the port declined, but Parkgate became established as a small seaside resort. In March 1988 Leyland Olympian DOG 181 (B181 BLG) is seen heading south along the sea front, the blind showing it to be working on Route 72C to Hooton Station, as it passes 'sister' bus DOG 137 (A137 SMA) on one of the few occasions in the year when water reached the promenade.

There is no water in sight on 21 January 2005 as First DAF/Ikarus 60022 (J423 NCP) passes the same spot, working Route 22A to Chester from West Kirby. *Keith Mason/JCH*

ROCK FERRY: On 7 October 1984 Bristol FS driver training bus G166 (CFM 901C) stands alongside Leyland Olympian DOG 140 (A140 SMA) at New Chester Road depot. Opened in 1932 with an allocation of 68, rising to 93 in 1965, then dropping to 77 in 1970, the depot was sold to PMT in 1990. The depot continues under First PMT, seen on 21 October 2004. *John Robinson/JCH*

TOLL BAR: A few miles south of Birkenhead, at New Ferry, both Crosville and Birkenhead Corporation had depots within a few hundred yards of one another. In our picture of 16 May 1964, Bristol MW EMG 352 (242 FFM) passes the Corporation garage working on Service F7 to Birkenhead. The sharp lines of an Austin A40 are unmistakeable.

The depot lasted until the early years of the PTE, approximately 1971. Not long afterwards it was demolished and a Post Office erected as seen in the photo of 21 October 2004. Arriva Volvo Olympian/Northern Counties Palatine 3299 (N299 CKB) is employed on the Wirral-Liverpool Cross River Express service. *A. J. Douglas/JCH*

WEST KIRBY is an attractive coastal town where the River Dee emerges from the estuary into the sea. Both a holiday and residential area, it enjoys good services by rail and bus to Liverpool on the other side of the Mersey. A long promenade offers fine views of Hilbre Island, with a large Marine Lake at the south end. In May 1987 Bristol VR DVL 405 (JMB 405T), new in 1979, stands outside the railway station terminus, working on Route 186 to Eastham Ferry. The bus displays the attractive Eagle Star logo advertisement (without wingtips!). The electric line serves all stations to Liverpool.

Despite several rain showers during 21 October 2004, it was dry when Arriva Volvo Olympian/Northern Counties Palatine 3302 (N302 CKB) was photographed in the same position on the express service to Liverpool via the Tunnel. *Keith Mason/JCH*

WEST KIRBY: Just over 50 years ago, on 7 August 1954, Bristol KSW MW423 (NFM 55) is about to leave for Moreton outside the attractive black and white building opposite the railway station. The vehicle was new to Crosville in 1951.

On 21 January 2005 Avon Buses-operated Dennis Dart/East Lancs 822 (X822 XCK) is seen working the similar Route 83 to Birkenhead via Moreton. The Dee Hotel is now part of the Wetherspoon Group. *N. R. Knight/JCH*

WEST KIRBY DEPOT: Opened in 1923 on the corner of Bridge Road and Orrysdale Road, the depot was built to hold 27 buses. The allocation in 1956 was 40, which remained consistent until slightly reduced to 38 in 1970. On 4 September 1983 several double-deckers can be seen – from left to right, they are Bristol VR DVL 329 (TMA 329R), together with Leyland Olympians DOG 105 (GFM 105X) and DOG 102 (GFM 102X).

In 1987 the garage was closed, but re-opened for minibuses for a period, finally closing in 1990. It was eventually demolished and the land sold for new housing, as seen in the photograph taken on 21 October 2004. The only point of contact between the 'past' and the 'present' is the church spire, which can just be seen above the roof of the depot in the older picture. *Both JCH*

WILLASTON is situated on the Wirral peninsula about halfway between Hooton and Neston. On 24 August 1981 Duple-bodied Leyland Leopard ELL 331 (JMB 331T) heads for Ellesmere Port sporting the TransPort livery, which was a consequence of the Market Analysis Project (MAP) and resulted in early days of 'branding' areas/routes.

Some 24 years later, on 21 January 2005, the attractive bus shelter remains, but is no longer in use. First DAF/Ikarus 60022 (J423 NCP) is employed on Route 22A to Chester from West Kirby. *Chris Lodington/JCH*

Liverpool area

Opposite LIVER BUILDING: Liverpool's waterfront is instantly recognisable, with the building displaying the two Liver Birds – known throughout the sea-going world. The city has many claims to fame, including two Cathedrals, two Premier League football clubs, the relatively new Albert Dock and, of course, the Beatles. It was a much sought-after destination for Crosville, although entry was resisted by Liverpool Corporation; however, in 1926, after considerable negotiation, Crosville buses were running into the city. This line-up of the company's buses at the Pier Head, together with a Liverpool tram, was photographed in August 1937.

The main buildings remain the same, but in the background beyond the Liver Buildings are a number of new ones, seen on 21 October 2004. The area to the left is where the ferries leave from and has been attractively opened out. Arriva Dennis Dart/Plaxton Pointer 2322 (T322 PNB) heads north along the waterfront. *G H F Atkins* © *John Banks Collection/JCH*

MANN ISLAND, near Pier Head, is where Bristol LD DLG 896 (853 AFM) was photographed on 30 June 1973, showing Prescot H11 on the blind. Bristol FLF DFG 249 (SFM 249F) is immediately behind.

On 21 October 2004 Arriva Dennis Dart/Plaxton Pointer 2285 (P419 HVX) awaits its next turn of duty on Route 14A to Kirkby. Above the driver's cab are the words '*Le bus* – going your way in Liverpool'. *John Robinson/JCH*

Opposite MANN ISLAND: On 11 July 1981 four Bristol VRs are seen at the terminus. The unusual architecture of the building in the background remains unchanged in the 'present' picture of 26 October 2004, with rather fewer buses on view – the nearest, a Leyland Lynx, having a driver under instruction. *A. Moyes/JCH*

LORD STREET: On 16 May 1986 Bristol VR DVL 363 (BTU 363S), working on Route H1, heads through the city centre with Radio City Tower beyond on the right. The latter was built in 1965, originally with a rotating restaurant; taken over by the local radio station in 1990, it is currently open to the public at weekends.

Only 18 years later on 29 November 2004 there has been a major change in this part of Lord Street: it is now pedestrianised, so buses heading towards the City Centre have to turn left into John Street. We therefore have to be content with a rear view of a GTL single-decker. The decoration across the street is probably part of the Christmas decorations but features Liverpool's 'Year of the Sea in 2005'. A curiosity is the arrow on the road to the right of the bus in what appears to be a one-way street – in the other direction! *Chris Lodington/JCH*

ST GEORGE'S HALL: This beautiful landmark in the City Centre, regarded as one of the finest neo-classical buildings in Europe, was completed in 1854. Built as law courts and as a venue for music festivals, it forms a wonderful backdrop to Bristol VR DVL 497 (WTU 497W) working on Route H25 on 24 June 1985.

By 29 November 2004 there is a different flow of traffic, but a constant stream of buses still passes the Hall, some turning into the nearby bus station in Roe Street. *Chris Lodington/JCH*

LIME STREET STATION: Bristol FLF coach DFB 149 (AFM 112B) is seen in Skelhorne Street by the side of the station after working in on Service X4 from Caernarfon on 28 January 1967, not long before the Beatles' classic *Penny Lane/Strawberry Fields Forever* **entered the pop charts.**

In the 'present' picture of 26 October 2004, Selwyns DAF/Wright Cadet X782 NWX has just pulled in with the Airport Express Route 500 to John Lennon Airport, named after the co-writer of those songs, at Speke. The modernisation of the station can be clearly seen behind the bus. *Chris Lodington/JCH*

QUEENSWAY MERSEY TUNNEL ENTRANCE: On 10 May 1989 Bristol VR DVL 339 (UMB 339R) had just emerged on the Liverpool side with Service 72A to Liverpool Exchange East terminus from Heswall via Arrowe Park Hospital. The tunnel was opened by King George V and Queen Mary on 18 July 1934.

On 26 October 2004 it appears that even the traffic cones remain in situ! First Volvo Olympian/Alexander 34228 (P228 MPU) arrives in Liverpool on the same route, photographed on 26 October 2004. *Chris Lodington/JCH*

RUNCORN: Although probably not widely known, Runcorn had a reputation as a spa town at the start of the 19th century, while quarrying was one of the first local industries. It expanded in the 1960s into a 'New Town', surrounded by hi-tech and chemical industries, and was a leading exponent of the construction of bus Expressways. In the 'past' picture, taken in 23 April 1980, two Crosville single-deckers are seen passing through Shopping City, with Bristol RE SRG 135 (DFM 135H) in the lead, showing Route T2 Norton Village on the blind.

Nearly 25 years later, on 8 February 2005, the scene has changed very little as an Arriva single-decker heads for Runcorn East, also showing Route 2. Buses stop at the North bus station, whereas on a parallel busway in the other direction the bus station is known as South. Shopping City has had a change of title to Halton Lea. *A. J. Douglas/JCH*

RUNCORN: With the impressive 'Jubilee' bridge in the background, Leyland National SNL 809 (WFM 809L) is working on a local service to the railway station on 28 February 1986. The bridge opened in 1961, replacing the Transporter Bridge that had lasted 56 years, having been the largest of its kind in the world. The bridge in the foreground is Waterloo Bridge, with its intricate metalwork.

Although the new bridge is obscured by trees, Waterloo Bridge is still unmistakable on 8 February 2005. To the left is the busy highway to and from the bridge over the Mersey, and on the right we see an Arriva single-decker heading for the town centre. *John Robinson/JCH*

SOUTHPORT is one of the three prime resorts of the Lancashire coast, with a great deal to offer visitors, from the Victorian elegance of tree-lined Lord Street, almost a mile of continuous shops, to the largest marine lake and the second longest seaside pier in the UK, a very popular amusement park and home to the famous annual Flower Show. On 4 August 1989 Plaxton-bodied Leyland Tiger CTL 35 (NLG 35Y) on Service X8 to Banks is seen in front of the building that was once the Cheshire Lines railway station, which closed in 1952. From 1954 to 1987 it was used as a bus station by Ribble, following which it was turned into an unsuccessful shopping centre.

On 29 November 2004 the arched entrance now bears the name of a well-known supermarket – Morrisons. At the busy bus stop we see Arriva Volvo/Wrightbus Renown 2728 (Y728 KNF), allocated to Southport garage, on Route 47 to Banks and Riverside Caravan Park. *John Robinson/JCH*

WAVERTREE: Passing the Leigh Arms in Picton Road on 21 June 1984, Bristol VR DVG 283 (MDM 283P) is working on the H8 route to Liverpool.

The Leigh Arms, no longer a public house, is now a studio, and has had new windows installed, but basically is much the same, including the ornamental wrought-iron work. Arriva Volvo/Wright Endurance 6592 (N592 CKA), working on Route 78, heads for the City Centre along this very busy road, having started its journey at Okell Drive near Halewood. *John Robinson/JCH*

Cheshire

ALDERLEY EDGE is an attractive village in a former copper-mining area, and has a number of claims to fame, including the old Mill at nearby Nether Alderley and the birthplace of author Alan Garner, while the Beckhams had a home here. For many years a bypass has been under consideration to relieve the traffic congestion from which the village suffers, but with no result as yet. On 30 July 1983 Bristol VR DVL 370 (BTU 370S) calls with Service 130, which runs between Manchester and Macclesfield.

In October 2004 the route was transferred to Arriva's Manchester depot, and on Sunday 10 October First Scania/Wright 61219 (YM52 UVR), on a rail substitute service between Manchester Piccadilly and Alderley, is at the Arriva stop, while Arriva Dennis Dart/Plaxton Pointer 858 (T528 AOB) passes en route to Macclesfield working on the same route as in the 'past' photo. *Both JCH*

ALTRINCHAM: Turning into the bus station on 3 December 1974 is ex-North Western Alexander-bodied Daimler Fleetline DDG 314 (JDB 249F) on Route E18.

Since the 'past' picture was taken, the area of the old bus station has been completely re-developed and a brand new Interchange in front of the railway station opened on the opposite side of the road. Apart from the rail service between Chester and Manchester (via Stockport), the station is one of the termini of the Metrolink tram system running to Bury via Manchester City Centre or to Piccadilly railway station. On 19 August 2004 Arriva Dennis Dart/Plaxton Pointer 1265 (K877 UDB) leaves the Interchange on service 13 to Trafford General Hospital.
A. J. Douglas/JCH

ALTRINCHAM: Bristol FS DFB 25 (635 LFM), new in 1960 and working Route 37 to Warrington, enters the busy main street at the start of its journey in August 1972.

This shopping area of the town has undergone complete re-development, as seen in the photograph of 19 August 2004. Heading in the Manchester direction is Stagecoach Volvo/Northern Counties 20881 (P881 MNE) on Route 371 (to Stockport), and to the right is the Interchange bus/rail station. Very few, if any, buses approach where the photographer was standing, as they all turn into the bus station entrance on the right beyond the overbridge. *Neville Knight/JCH*

BOLLINGTON has an industrial history long associated with the textile industry, but is now a pleasant dormitory for Macclesfield and other towns. It boasts a remarkably long main street that is a perfect example of 'ribbon' development. Standing at the terminus on 27 February 1972 is SRL 257 (SJA 392K), a Bristol RE that had been ordered by North Western but was delivered to Crosville following transfer of the business that same year. Originally in NW livery, it was re-painted by Crosville before entering service. It is working on Route 57, which runs between Moss Rose Estate and Bollington/Pott Shrigley.

At the time of the 'present' picture, Service 192 was operated by Arriva from its Macclesfield garage. Dennis Dart/Plaxton Pointer 867 (X217 JOF) was photographed on 2 September 2004 shortly before the return journey. Apart from the modern bus shelter and considerable tree growth, there has been little change. *Neville Knight/JCH*

BREDBURY parking ground opened in 1986 when Route 197 was commenced between Stockport and Manchester, as an outstation to Macclesfield. In August 1987, in addition to Ford bowser UTJ 466H there are two Bristol VRs present and two Leyland Nationals.

The area passed to Bee Line in November 1989, and when visited on 10 February 2005 nothing remained to link the past with the present except the open area, which now belongs to Tarmac. *A. Moyes/JCH*

BROKEN CROSS, near Macclesfield, is on the A537 between Monks Heath and Macclesfield. Ex-North Western Alexander-bodied Leyland Leopard CLL 925 (FJA 219D) is seen on 20 May 1978 heading towards the town centre on Route E26; in the 1977 timetable this service ran between Northwich and Macclesfield, with only a couple of journeys each day.

The 'present' photograph was taken on 30 December 2004 and, as can be seen, there have been some changes to the buildings, although the nearest cluster of chimney pots remains the same. A pedestrian crossing has been added, together with a roundabout. Arriva Dennis Dart/Northern Counties Paladin 1142 (L116 YVK) is seen entering the main road en route to Manchester working on Route 130. *P. J. Thompson/JCH*

CHEADLE: On 21 September 1974 Bristol FLF DFB 115 (148 YFM) is seen taking the right turn into High Street on the E30 service, which operated between Macclesfield and Manchester. The bus would be allocated to Macclesfield garage.

Although the same route continues to be operated by Arriva (now 129/130), in the 'present' photograph, taken on 25 August 2004, we see new Scania/East Lancs MX04 MYW on locally based operator Bullock's service 157, which runs between Woodford and Manchester. *Neville Knight/JCH*

CONGLETON has a long history of lace-making and leather-working, then silk and cotton weaving, and it is known that there was a market held here as long ago as 1386. Crosville inherited the local services from North Western, and in 1980 opened an outstation to Macclesfield depot, based at the Cattle Market outside the town, following the closure of Biddulph garage. On 21 August 1983 Bristol VR DVL 491 (WTU 491W) is seen outside the Portakabin office. Peeping round the back, acting as a store shed, is Bristol LH SLP 153 (DFM 153H) – new to Crosville in 1970 – together with a Ford tanker vehicle.

On 29 September 2004 the only remaining evidence is the Portakabin, the area now being used as a trailer park. *Both JCH*

CREWE has several claims to fame. Established by the Grand Junction Railway in 1837, it was the London & North Western Railway that made it a true 'Railway Town', centred at the junction of six main lines, and with one of the largest locomotive works in the country. It was also the original home of the world-famous Rolls-Royce cars. In more recent times it carries the deserved reputation for its floral decorations. On 9 August 1953 Bristol K6B MW 412 (KFM 288) is seen outside the railway station on local Service 207 to Mablins Lane.

Over half a century later, on 4 October 2004, First PMT Leyland Olympian 30076 (B199 DTU), employed on Route 20 from Kidsgrove to Crewe, has just pulled out from the station stop. This bus had been new to Crosville as DOG 199. *Neville Knight/JCH*

CREWE: Opened in 1960, following closure of Queen Street, in 1970 Delamere Street depot/bus station had an allocation of 64 vehicles. On 7 March 1985 dual-doored Bristol RE SRG 194 (HFM 194J), new in 1970, is seen turning into its stand on local Service K14. In 1989 the depot was transferred to Midland Red North.

In the 'present' photo, dated 4 October 2004, Arriva Dennis Dart/Plaxton Pointer 872 (Y32 TDA) is operating on Route 6 to Leighton Hospital. Apart from the present ownership by Arriva North West & Wales, there has been virtually no change in the passing of nearly 20 years. *John Robinson/JCH*

48

CREWE: A further view of the area shows part of the length of the garage, down one side of the bus station. On 21 August 1983 among the Leyland Nationals is, second from the left, SNL 583 (JTU 583T).

Just over 21 years later, on 4 October 2004, the only apparent difference is that the buses are Arriva with Leyland Lynx 1747 (G327 NUM) on the left and First PMT Dennis Dart/Plaxton (M961 XVT) on the right of the picture. *Both JCH*

CREWE: In Market Street in about 1958 we see a study in styles – on the left is 1954 Bristol LD ML 686 (RFM 431) and on the right Bristol K6B MW 402 (KFM 278), four years its senior, with the driver leaning across to speak to his colleague.

On 28 September 2004 we can see that the rather ornately designed building with the stonework stripes remains in situ, but the one beyond has been replaced by a modern structure without character. Arriva Leyland Lynx 1748 (H408 YMA) on Service 84 approaches the terminus. *John Fozard/JCH*

CREWE: This busy scene in the Market Square was photographed in the late 1950s and depicts buses using the Square as the terminus prior to the opening of the new bus station in 1960. A Bristol K is on the left in front of the Odeon cinema, a Bristol LD Lodekka to its right, and two more Bristol Ks on the extreme right.

As seen in the present-day view on 4 October 2004, the tower and main buildings remain much the same, but over to the left the Odeon has been demolished. To the right of the War Memorial we catch a glimpse of an Arriva bus having just left the bus station on the other side of the tower. *Cheshire & Chester Archives & Local Studies/JCH*

FRODSHAM: The Mersey estuary is close by and in medieval times there was a thriving port here, used to send local cheese and salt to Liverpool. A very wide and long main street allows a flourishing market to take place each week. New in 1979, Leyland National SNL 674 (MCA 674T) is employed on Route E47, which ran between Northwich and Frodsham.

Quite a lot of rebuilding and refurbishment has gone on but basically the scene is much the same on 21 January 2005, looking east, as First 30068 (A170 VFM) passes by. This Leyland Olympian is a former Crosville vehicle (DOG 170), new in 1984 and transferred to PMT in February 1990. *Chris Lodington/JCH*

FRODSHAM: Just to the east of the village, the A56 crosses the Weaver Navigation by the Sutton Weaver swing bridge. Rising in the Peckforton Hills, the waterway was used to carry salt down river and later chemicals from the newly developed industry. In October 1982 Bristol VR DVL 372 (BTU 372S) comes over the swing bridge towards Frodsham, working on Route C31 from Warrington to Chester. The control cabin for the bridge is on the left.

Visually very little has changed on 21 January 2005, nearly 23 years later, as Arriva Scania/Northern Counties Paladin 1050 (P250 NBA) is likewise employed on a Chester service. *Keith Mason/JCH*

HALE has long been considered an attractive residential area where in the past wealthy Manchester textile merchants lived. The railway came early to the village in the form of the Cheshire Midland (later to be part of the Cheshire Lines Committee), and the station was opened in 1862. On 23 September 1978 Bristol RE SRL 258 (SJA 393K), ordered by North Western but delivered after Crosville had taken over, passes the signal box working on Route E69 to Alderley Edge.

It is interesting that Route E69 is still in existence in 2004, worked by Whitegate Travel, operating a single journey in each direction two days a week between Altrincham and Alderley Edge. On 16 December Arriva Dennis Dart/East Lancs 1217 (M217 AKB) is employed on Route 288 between Altrincham and Knutsford via Wilmslow. Although the signal box has been closed for some years, it has been maintained in excellent external condition. *P. J. Thompson/JCH*

HALE BARNS lies between Altrincham and Wilmslow on the A538. On 26 September 1977 another Bristol RE, ordered by North Western, SRL 256 (SJA 391K), is working on Route E17, which ran from Altrincham to Macclesfield via Wilmslow and Prestbury.

The 'present' photograph, taken on 16 December 2004, shows that the building on the right-hand side has been demolished and a terrace of town houses built, but the church of Holy Angels, with its unusual tower, stands proudly on the corner. Arriva Dennis Dart/Alexander 2309 (R309 CVU) is employed on the Altrincham to Manchester Airport Route 19A. *P. J. Thompson/JCH*

HAZEL GROVE: The Five Ways is a busy junction on the A523 between Stockport and Macclesfield, and gives its name to the adjacent public house. Leyland National SNG 397 (KMA 397T), sporting the 'Lynx' motif, waits for the lights to change while operating on Route E8 to Macclesfield from Stockport, which took in Poynton, Pott Shrigley and Bollington, on 3 October 1986.

On 23 December 2004 Stotts of Oldham's Mercedes-Benz/Plaxton Beaver KE53 HGP is working the Stockport to Bramhall Route 390. The company also runs Route 307, which is a Stockport circular taking in Cheadle Heath, Cheadle, Cheadle Hulme and Bramhall. Buses come over from and return to Oldham each day. *P. J. Thomson/JCH*

HIGHER POYNTON: In the summer of 1978 ex-North Western Marshall-bodied Bristol RE SRG 231 (KJA 308G) is seen working on Route E8 (Macclesfield-Stockport), not having strayed far from its origins.

Despite the 30-odd years between the 'past' and 'present' pictures, the scene has changed very little. Stagecoach Mercedes-Benz Vario/Plaxton Beaver 42568 (R277 CBU), ex-Glossopdale, approaches on what is now Route 191, which operates between Middlewood and Stockport, extended to Manchester at peak times. *Neville Knight/JCH*

KNUTSFORD: Made famous by Mrs Gaskell's book *Cranford*, which was based on the town, Knutsford has retained its old world charm, but is an excellent shopping centre. Its close proximity to Tatton Park brings many visitors to the area. In the photograph of August 1987, Leyland National SNG 867 (PFM 867M) awaits its next turn of duty in the bus station on Service E28, together with Shearings Leyland National 70 (NWT 720M). The building behind is the rear of the Crown Court.

Today now primarily a car park for a supermarket, the whole area was once part of the town gaol, which in the mid-19th century held 700-plus prisoners and where seven executions were carried out. Photographed on 18 October 2004, nearby is the small modern bus station. *John Robinson/JCH*

KNUTSFORD: In around 1978, by which time Leyland Nationals had been delivered in good numbers, we see ENL 936 (HMA 657N) passing the down-side buildings of the ex-Cheshire Lines Committee station (dating back to 1863) on the E68 route to Wilmslow.

The scene has hardly altered in the 25 years to 5 September 2004 apart from a new building across the line. There have been a few minor changes to the station premises, which are now privately occupied. Arriva Dennis Dart/Carlyle Dartline 1132 (G122 RGT) is seen on Route 300, which is the Knutsford circular. *John Robinson/JCH*

MACCLESFIELD: Situated in the foothills of the Pennines, the history of the town is very much bound up with textiles, and the silk industry in particular, having become the principal centre in the country for silk-weaving and also for the manufacture of silk-covered buttons. In 1974, with the spire of St Paul's Church visible in the background, ex-North Western Alexander-bodied Daimler Fleetline DDG 308 (FJA 195D) passes Park Green on the Route E20 Weston Estate service, having come down Sunderland Street from the bus station. This vehicle remained in service until the early 1980s.

The scene had not changed greatly when the 'present' shot was taken on 5 September 2004, other than the tree growth. Since the new bus station was opened, very few buses pass along Sunderland Street from the direction of the garage, so we have to be content with the rear of Arriva Dennis Dart/Plaxton Pointer 857 (T527 AOB) on Route 9 as it makes its way to the bus station. *Neville Knight/JCH*

MACCLESFIELD: Caught on camera on 19 May 1973 as it turns out of the bus station into Sunderland Street, Bristol LD DLB 899 (881 CFM) is in use on Route E21, which ran between Weston Estate and Hurdsfield Industrial Estate.

By 5 September 2004 the bus station has been moved nearer the town centre, although the garage remains. No service buses pass the railway station (seen on the right) coming towards the photographer, but Arriva Dennis Dart/East Lancs 1149 (L618 BNX) is en route to the new terminus. The building on the right has undergone some modification but basically things are much the same. The coaches seen in the background are on hire to Network Rail during part of the engineering blockade affecting the Stoke line. *Neville Knight/JCH*

MACCLESFIELD: On 30 July 1983 Leyland National SNL 882 (RFM 882M) is employed on Route E11 to Moss Rose Estate as the driver prepares for the right turn into the bus station. This bus was new in 1974 and had a Gardner engine fitted in 1982 when it was re-designated to SNG, but the fleet number had not been amended on the bus when photographed.

There have been no great changes in the intervening 21 years to 6 August 2004 as Arriva Dennis Dart/Plaxton Pointer 867 (X217 JOF) is about to take a left turn towards the new bus station, on Service 10 (also to Moss Rose Estate). The use of a wide-angle lens allows us to see the area around the Parish Church, although considerable tree growth now hides most of the east end. *Both JCH*

MACCLESFIELD: Sunderland Street Depot became part of Crosville following the break up of North Western on 1 January 1972. In the 'past' photo of 23 October 1982 there is a Bristol VR inside, and the rear of Bristol MW recovery vehicle G427 (808 FFM) can be seen in the left side of the doorway. Although some way from the town centre, the site also contained the town's bus station.

After the end of Crosville in 1990, the depot was taken over by C-Line and Bee Line, then Midland Red North, then Stevensons, until finally becoming Arriva. In the first half of 2004 a new bus station was built nearer the town and Sunderland Street became the garage only, as seen on 6 August 2004, with the bus station area now used for parking employees' cars. Only the name above the door has changed!

Subsequently it was announced that the garage would close and the buildings would be demolished for development. The allocation would be reduced to 10 buses for local services, and Manchester depot would operate the E30 to Macclesfield. There would be a new base at Lyme Green (subsequently to become an outstation to Crewe). The third picture shows the outcome, with rapid demolition having taken place by 30 December 2004. *All JCH*

MIDDLEWICH is one of the historic salt towns of Cheshire, perhaps today better known as a canal centre on the Trent & Mersey Navigation. Leyland Nationals SNL 815 (WFM 815L) and SNL 986 (YTU 986S) pass one another near the centre of the town on 18 October 1984, operating on Route K37.

The main route through the town remains the 37, as Arriva Mercedes-Benz Vario/Alexander 388 (P58 HOJ) was photographed heading for Sandbach Common on 19 February 2005. The building on the right is no longer a newsagent, but otherwise little has changed. The wide-angle lens brings the Parish Church into the picture. *John Robinson/JCH*

MOBBERLEY: About halfway between Knutsford and Wilmslow, Leyland National SNL 404 (KMA 404T) stops at the 'Bird in Hand' on Route E68 on 14 May 1983. The vehicle was allocated to Macclesfield depot.

Just over 21 years later, on 22 September 2004, Arriva Dennis Dart/East Lancs 1257 (N257 CKA) working the same service (now the 288, which runs from Knutsford to Altrincham via Wilmslow) passes the pub, which has a beautiful inn sign of a peregrine falcon. *Both JCH*

NANTWICH DEPOT was built to house nine buses, and opened in 1915. By 1947 the allocation had increased to 17, but in 1962 came closure. In the 'past' photo, taken in October 1985, the buildings were in private use.
   Eventually the land was sold and re-developed as a Safeway supermarket and car park, as seen on 7 April 2004, the two pictures securely 'locked' together by the building beyond. *A. Moyes/JCH*

NORTHWICH's depot and bus station at Chester Way were taken over by Crosville on the break-up of North Western in 1972. On 19 June 1983 a line-up of vehicles from both companies includes, from right to left, Bristol REs SRL 253 (SJA 388K), SRL 252 (SJA 387K), both ex-North Western, VR DVL 428 (RLG 428V), REs CRL 259 (TFM 259K) and SRL 248 (SJA 383K), and MW recovery vehicle G409 (429 UFM). In 1980 the allocation was 50 vehicles.

Following the closure of the depot, the area has been completely re-developed, primarily as a Kwik-Save supermarket, as seen in the 'present' photo of 1 November 2004. *Both JCH*

NORTHWICH BUS STATION: The town is one of the salt towns of the county at the confluence of the Rivers Weaver and Dane, and Britain's only Salt Museum is located here. A substantial chemical business also developed in the area. In a busy scene on 14 February 1987, two 'Mini Lynx' Freight Rover Sherpas, the right-hand one being MSR 770 (D770 PTU), new in 1986, a Bristol VR and a Leyland National are visible. After the area was sold for redevelopment, the buses were transferred to Winsford.

Although the bus station no longer exists, at least we can link the 'past' with the 'present' by the building on the opposite side of Chester Way and the church steeple just to the left of the trees, as seen on 1 November 2004. The road had been temporarily made into one-way until Hayhurst Bridge re-opened. Arriva Dennis Dart/Plaxton Pointer 869 (X32 KON) is in dedicated Route 1 livery. *John Robinson/JCH*

NORTHWICH: On 16 May 1973 ex-North Western Park Royal-bodied AEC Renown DAA 510 (VDB 975), incoming from Weaverham, crosses the Weaver Navigation at Hayhurst Bridge on Chester Way.
    The bridge had been closed for a period due to the discovery of major corrosion, which explains the barriers seen in the photo of 1 November 2004, although it was getting close to re-opening. It was the first of the electric swing bridges in the area. *A. Moyes/JCH*

NORTHWICH: Ex-North Western Bristol RE SRL 250 (SJA 385K) climbs the hill at Winnington towards Barnton on 29 September 1984 employed on Route E54. There is a heavily industrialised background of mainly chemical works, including that of Brunner Mond (part of ICI), which manufactured a variety of products, including calcium chloride, soda ash and sodium bicarbonate.

On 1 November 2004 Arriva Dennis Dart/Plaxton Pointer 862 (X212 JOF) is working on the Barnton circular Route 1 and is seen in the same position as the 'past' picture. However, there have been considerable changes in the background as many of the buildings in the complex have been demolished, including a liquid caustic works, and a new one erected. *A. Moyes/JCH*

NORTHWICH: On 30 April 1976 Bristol RE coach CRG 572 (HFM 572D) crosses the swing bridge at Barnton Cut, near Winnington, working on Route 851 to London. This National Express service started in Liverpool (at the ferries), then went via Speke Airport, Hunts Cross, Halewood, Widnes and Runcorn to Northwich, then Middlewich and non-stop to Hendon and London. Less than a mile away is the famous Anderton Lift on the Trent & Mersey Canal.

The 'present' photo taken on 1 November 2004 shows very little change as Arriva Dennis Dart/Plaxton Pointer 869 (X32 KON), on the Barnton Circular service, crosses the bridge. *John Robinson/JCH*

STOCKPORT: Ex-Crosville Leyland Olympian DOG 110 (GFM 110X), new in 1982, is seen at the bus station on 4 February 1991 on route 197 (Hazel Grove to Manchester Victoria), after the vehicle had been transferred to Bee Line in November 1989.

Bee Line may have gone, but the Hat Museum stands proudly in the background! Stagecoach is now the dominant bus company in the area, and on 25 August 2004 Leyland Olympian/Northern Counties 13155 (B155 XNA) waits for departure time on Route 383, the Stockport to Romiley Circular. *John Robinson/JCH*

STOCKPORT: Bristol RE SRL 258 (SJA 393K), ordered by North Western but delivered to CMS, climbs out of Mersey Square in June 1973 on Route E8 to Macclesfield. In the background can be seen several SELNEC double-deckers and the Victorian viaduct that carries the main line to Manchester.

Mersey Square itself is no longer the terminus, as the new bus station was built nearby, but St Petersgate is still used by many services leaving the town and heading south. On 7 October 2004 Trent Barton Optare Excel 189 (T789 XVO) is en route to Buxton having come from Manchester Airport on Route 199. The background chimney has gone and a modern building has been added near the viaduct. *John Robinson/JCH*

THELWALL is probably best known for the delays on the nearby M6 viaduct! On 1 August 1987 Bristol VR DVL 381 (FTU 381T), delivered in 1978, passes Thelwall Post Office on the right and the Pickering Arms on the opposite side, en route between Warrington and Altrincham (Service 37), formerly a North Western service.

A small unspoiled village just off the beaten track, little has changed here in the intervening 17 years to 18 October 2004. Served by both Arriva and Warrington Borough Transport, we see Dennis Dart/Northern Counties 230 (L230 SWM) of the latter working on Route 5, the Warrington-Warburton service. *John Robinson/JCH*

WILMSLOW: From a quiet village in the mid-1950s, Wilmslow had grown to a busy town by the turn of the 21st century. The transformation probably started when the well-known department store of Finnigans moved out of Manchester to Wilmslow, which became a very popular shopping destination. Its greatest claim to fame, however, was the discovery of 'Lindow Man' in a nearby peat bog in 1983. Green buses first appeared in Wilmslow following the demise of North Western in 1972, and the transfer of Macclesfield garage to Crosville. On 30 July 1983 Leyland National SNL 886 (RFM 886M) is seen in Swan Street with an E17 service to Macclesfield from Altrincham. The bus was new to Crosville in 1974.

Around 20 years later, on 26 August 2004, there has been continued building re-development, and the bank on the right behind the bus has changed name from Midland to HSBC. Arriva Dennis Dart/Northern Counties Paladin 1122 (L126 YVK) is employed on the important Route 130 between Macclesfield and Manchester. *Both JCH*

WILMSLOW: Leyland National SNL 983 (YTU 983S) is working the E67 Wilmslow Circular in Bank Square on 6 August 1983. The building on the right was the local police station at the time, subsequently to become a pub called 'The Blue Lamp'.

That building was subsequently demolished, and with new buildings going up in its place on 10 August 2004 Baker's of Biddulph Mercedes-Benz/Plaxton Beaver 180 (V116 ESL) is seen on Route 34 to Congleton, which calls in at Astra Zeneca at Alderley Park. *Both JCH*

Manchester and Lancashire

MANCHESTER PICCADILLY: The history of the city dates back to the Roman occupation of Mancunium, but it was in Victorian times that it grew as a major centre of commerce and industry, particularly in cotton. The Ship Canal, opening in 1894, turned Manchester into a major inland port. There are a number of fine buildings, including the magnificent Gothic Town Hall, while music has also played a big part in the city's cultural development, the Free Trade Hall being the home of the Hallé Orchestra and in modern times the building of the Bridgewater Hall keeping the tradition alive. Two Premiership football teams both enjoy great support. Crosville was a late-comer – not until the break-up of North Western were its green buses a daily occurrence. On 14 January 1990 Bristol VR DVL 430 (RLG 430V) is seen at the bus station showing route 167 on the blind. Although still carrying the Crosville name, the vehicle had officially been transferred to Bee Line on 25 November 1989. On the right is Bee Line Roe-bodied Atlantean 1629 (LCD 43P) on Route 97 to Bury Interchange.

The bus station has undergone various changes over the years – now Stagecoach dominates, but it is also used by Arriva, Bullocks and Finglands among others. Off camera to the left in our 'present' picture, taken on 16 August 2004, is the Metrolink tram line. A Stagecoach Alexander-bodied Dennis Trident is on Route 255, which operates between Manchester and Partington, and behind to the left is another Stagecoach vehicle in 'Magic Bus' livery. *John Robinson/JCH*

MANCHESTER, PORTLAND STREET: Bristol FLF DFG 254 (SFM 254F) heads out of the City Centre working on Route E29 to Macclesfield at about 11 o'clock on Sunday morning 12 June 1977, hence the lack of traffic.

On 6 January 2005 there is rather more activity with First Scania/Wright 60187 (V135 DND) en route to Leigh on Service 39, followed by a Stagecoach double-decker, behind which is a shuttle bus from Piccadilly railway station to Deansgate and return. One large and not very attractive building has been added on Piccadilly, otherwise there is little change. *P. J. Thompson/JCH*

MANCHESTER, CHORLTON STREET: Using a temporary terminus, ex-North Western Alexander-bodied Dennis Loline DEG 402 (RDB 897) awaits departure time to Macclesfield on Route 30 on 17 June 1975. Chorlton Street bus station is below the multi-storey car park on the left.

A new service is the Stagecoach Megabus to London, seen on 6 January 2005, with three-axle Leyland Olympian/Alexander 13626 (H41 GBD), from Hong Kong. The journey takes 4½ hours with a single fare from $5, or even less. *P. J. Thompson/JCH*

MANCHESTER, SACKVILLE STREET: Just across the road from Chorlton Street bus station, on 22 September 1983, Plaxton-bodied Bristol RE ERL 295 (BFM 295L) lays over before returning to Aberystwyth on long-distance Service X8. This was a 'Town Lynx' service that ran via Machynlleth, Newtown, Welshpool, Oswestry, Wrexham, Chester and Altrincham, taking exactly 5 hours.

In the 'present' shot we have a line-up of UK North double-deckers waiting their next turn of duty, with Leyland Olympian/East Lancs 214 (R371 DJN) at the front, on 12 October 2004. There has been considerable tree growth in the 21 years between the two photographs. *Both JCH*

MANCHESTER VICTORIA: With the ex-Lancashire & Yorkshire Railway station in the background, Bristol VR DVL 414 (ODM 414V) awaits its time of departure on Service 197 to Stockport on 16 August 1986. To accommodate this newly won route, Crosville opened an out-station at Bredbury. It may have been that no terminus position could be found in the increasingly congested Piccadilly, hence the unusual choice of Victoria for the terminus.

Today things are very different in so much that apart from the free shuttle bus round central Manchester, only a few buses pass in front of the station, and these are during the evening rush hour. We see First Optare Solo 40333 (ML02 OGC) working Metroshuttle Route 2 on 12 October 2004. To the left are the steps leading to the Arena entertainment centre. *Nigel Chatfield/JCH*

MANCHESTER, ST PETER'S SQUARE: In driving sleet and snow on the afternoon of 27 November 1985, outside the Central Library, Bristol VR DVL 414 (ODM 414V) enters Mosley Street, working on Route 129. This vehicle joined Bee Line in November 1989.

The weather was rather better on 6 January 2005, with little change in the surrounding buildings, but there is a newcomer on the block in the shape of Metrolink trams running through the square. In front of the Library is Bullock of Cheadle's East Lancs-bodied Dennis Trident W674 PTD working on Service 42 to East Didsbury, a route shared by several other companies. *P. J. Thompson/JCH*

PARRS WOOD, East Didsbury, had two claims to transport fame. It was at one time the municipal tram terminus for the line that ran down the centre of Kingsway out of Manchester, and it was also the home of a large Manchester Corporation bus garage. On 13 May 1974 Bristol LD DLB 899 (881 CFM), new in 1957, is operating on Route E30 from Manchester to Macclesfield, as it passes the old depot and turns right into Kingsway heading for Cheadle.

Following closure of the depot it was used for a period as a centre for Ford Trucks, before being bought by Tesco, who built a large supermarket and car park, but left the clock tower in situ. On 6 January 2005 UK North DAF/Ikarus 100 (M605 RCP) makes the right turn in order to access the bus station. *P. J. Thompson/JCH*

ROCHDALE is famed for the start of the Co-operative Movement in Toad Lane, its Gothic Town Hall and, of course, as the birthplace of Gracie Fields. Yelloway Motor Services was a very successful coach company based in the town until, following the retirement of the son of the original owner, it was sold, then followed a sad tale of decline. Ending up in the same group as Crosville, the latter was to absorb Yelloway in 1988 – at which time limited stage carriage services were still being operated with a deteriorating fleet of buses. The garage was close to the centre of the town in Weir Street, and our 'past' photo shows the depot holding Crosville buses in January 1989, not long before Crosville itself was broken up.

The building was soon demolished and the photo of 27 January 2005 shows that it is now a car park. The curious semi-circular protrusion in the road edge on the right-hand side 'locks' the two photos together. *Malcolm Jones/JCH*

WARRINGTON is a bustling town on the River Mersey with an industrial heritage that continues into modern times. There are fine examples of Georgian architecture and in front of the Town Hall are some wonderful ornamental cast-iron gates, made at Ironbridge and originally intended for Sandringham. The bus depot was opened in 1924 in Chester New Road, and in the 'past' photo, taken on 7 August 1978, there are two Bristol Lodekkas, with DFG 170 (BFM 889B) in the front, awaiting their next turns of duty.

The Parish Church of St James Latchford on Wilderspool Causeway remains as a permanent link with the past. On 8 February 2005 a Halton Transport Dennis Dart passes by. *John Robinson/JCH*

Below At the nearby Arpley bus station is 1948 Bedford-Beadle chassisless MO19 (JFM 991), which had been converted into a mobile office, as seen in 1969. *John Robinson Collection*

WARRINGTON: On 10 August 1985 Bristol LH SLL 628 (OCA 628P) passes the Royal Oak public house in Bridge Street, with the conveniently situated Bible Book Shop next door.

Much remains the same almost 20 years later on 8 February 2005 as Warrington Borough Transport Dennis Dominator/East Lancs 102 (C102 UBC) approaches the major junction showing Route 5A to Wilderspool. *John Robinson/JCH*

WIDNES was a town that became a large industrialised area on the River Mersey, specialising in the chemical industry. It was also an important staging post for Crosville, ultimately allowing the company to run services into Liverpool. On 11 April 1989 Bristol VR DVL 391 (FTU 391T) is seen leaving the town en route to Runcorn on Service H25, one of a group of services that operated between Warrington and Liverpool (with intermediate variations). By the end of November of that year this bus had been transferred to the re-formed North Western, heralding the final demise of Crosville.

The buildings on the right-hand side are much the same, as seen on 8 February 2005, but the road formation has changed, no longer being a roundabout, with an area for car parking having been created. On the left-hand side a Halton Transport Dennis Dart is working to Runcorn on Route 61. *John Young/JCH*

Derbyshire

BUXTON: Famous for its thermal baths, the highest market in England, and surrounded by the beautiful Peak District, the town has a great deal to offer visitors. At the outer limits of the post-deregulation Crosville empire, on a wintry 26 February 1989, Bristol VR DVL 490 (WTU 490W), which was new in 1981, is employed on Route 199 (Stockport-Buxton-Burbage) awaiting departure time from Market Square. This route was operated by Crosville on Sundays only, using vehicles from Bredbury. Later in the year the bus was transferred to Bee Line.

The 'present' picture was taken on 7 October 2004, as Trent Barton 'Skyline'-branded Optare Excel 209 (V209 ENU) shows the same route as the 'past' picture, which today is between Derby/Buxton, Stockport and Manchester Airport. *John Robinson/JCH*

Shropshire

OSWESTRY is a busy market town close to the Welsh border, and the birthplace of the poet Wilfred Owen. Prosperity came in the 1860s when the Cambrian Railways established their headquarters here, and although the railway closed in 1966 the impressive station building has survived. In June 1984 Bristol VR DVG 466 (WTU 466W) is working on Route D2 to Chester, which ran via Gobowen (railway station) and Wrexham.

The parked cars made it difficult to match the shot exactly in February 2005. Arriva Dennis Dart/Plaxton Pointer 2297 (BF52 NZP) is working on Route 402 to Middleton Road. *A. Moyes/JCH*

OSWESTRY DEPOT was acquired together with Western Transport in 1933, and by 1947 there was an allocation of 14 vehicles, rising to 24 by 1980. Our photograph shows the premises on 8 October 1982, with Bristol RE SRG 113 (AFM 113G) showing 'School Bus', Route D65, waiting its next turn of duty. In 1986 the garage and operations passed to Crosville Wales, despite being in the English county of Shropshire, and continued as such until vacated in 1999, by which time it had passed to Midland Red North. Buses were then transferred to an industrial building on Salop Road, although it was unable to accommodate double-deckers, and the operation is now part of Arriva.

Since then the site has been re-developed into an Aldi supermarket and car park, as seen on 7 April 2004. The bus station lies beyond the fencing. *A. Moyes/JCH*

SHREWSBURY is a delightful town built in a loop of the River Severn, with a long history dating back to the time of William the Conqueror and a fine array of timber-framed buildings. In May 1986 Leyland National SNG 411 (LMA 411T) stands at the Barker Street bus station employed on Route D75 to Newtown.

Eighteen years later, on 21 September 2004, the introduction of a one-way system and the new bus station at Smithfield Road has eliminated Barker Street as a bus terminus. Probably no service buses pass on their way to the town centre, and it was fortunate to get Shearings Volvo 503 (MX03 AAK) offering a token presence! *Malcolm Jones/JCH*

WHITCHURCH is a busy market town, birthplace of the composer Edward German and home of J. B. Joyce, the well-known manufacturer of railway and tower clocks. In September 1977 Bristol RE SRG 212 (HFM 212J), from Crewe depot, leaves for Cholmondeley (pronounced 'Chumley'!) on Service K65. For a period Crosville outstationed vehicles at Salopia's garage in the town.

Following re-development with car parks, supermarket, etc, a small bus station was included in the plans. In the 'present' picture of 3 February 2005 the approach road is unrecognisable – the only landmark is the church, to the immediate left of the Tesco building, which on this morning was barely visible due to misty drizzle!
A. Moyes/JCH

Staffordshire

BIDDULPH is well known for the nearby National Trust Biddulph Grange Garden. Crosville came to the town with the break-up of North Western in 1972, when it inherited the shared garage (with PMT). In the 'past' photo of 19 April 1976, Bristol LH SLL 622 (OCA 622P) stands in front of the depot with ex-North Western CLL 923 (FJA 215D) to the rear. On the left is a PMT Bristol RE 227 with an ex-North Western AEC Renown Alexander-bodied Leyland Leopard behind it inside the depot.

Following closure in 1980, the area has been re-developed and there are flats now where the garage once stood, as seen on 12 March 2005. *A. Moyes/JCH*

NEWCASTLE-UNDER-LYME is an ancient borough that has maintained its independence from nearby Stoke-on-Trent. There has been a great deal of re-development in the town, but a number of older buildings have survived, including the Guildhall, which dates back to 1713. In the 'past' photo of 17 July 1986 Leyland National ENL 826 (NFM 826M) leaves the bus station working on Route K66 to Knighton.

The area has been completely re-built and there is no visual link with the past. On 12 March 2005 First Scania 65707 (YN04 GNG) is leaving the busy modern bus station, which is dominated by First PMT. To the right is an Arriva single-decker working on Route 64 to Shrewsbury. *John Robinson/JCH*

Yorkshire

HALIFAX's prosperity was based on wool, and Piece Hall, built in 1779, was the market place for the surrounding cottage wool industry. Later the Industrial Revolution and the advent of steam power were instrumental in the opening of many mills. The town was perhaps not the most likely terminus of a Crosville route, but after it took over the remains of Yelloway, Crosville found itself with regular trips over the Pennines on Service 556 between Halifax and Manchester. On 28 January 1989 Leyland National SNG 340 (CFM 340S) is seen working to Manchester via Ripponden and Oldham, as it passes the then Headquarters of the Halifax Building Society. The bus was new to Crosville in 1978.

When visited on 27 January 2005 there was no shortage of buses to be photographed in the same position. The principal change is that the Halifax Building Society has opened a new HQ in the town, but in its still-owned building there are stickers in the windows advertising a 'Loan Sale'! First Dennis Lance/Plaxton Verde 60991 (N453 JUG) is working on Route 503 to Huddersfield. *John Young/JCH*

Index of locations

CHESTER: It is perhaps fitting that the last photograph is of one of the remaining reminders of Crosville, the name still to be seen on 15 August 2004 by 'The Rink' in Liverpool Road. *JCH*